The Woman with a Cat on Her Shoulder
and Other Riffs

Books by Richard Katrovas

Green Dragons
Snug Harbor
The Public Mirror
The Book of Complaints
Prague, USA
Dithyrambs
Mystic Pig
The Republic of Burma Shave
Prague Winter
The Years of Smashing Bricks: An Anecdotal Memoir
Scorpio Rising: Selected Poems
Raising Girls in Bohemia: Meditations of an American Father
Swastika into Lotus
The Great Czech Navy
Poets and the Fools Who Love Them: A Memoir in Essays

The Woman with a Cat on Her Shoulder and Other Riffs

Richard Katrovas

Carnegie Mellon University Press
Pittsburgh 2022

Acknowledgments

Grateful acknowledgment is made to the editors of the following publications, where these poems, or slightly altered versions of them, first appeared:

Crosswinds: "A Riff on Identity Politics and MLK"
Ekphrastic Review: "The Woman with a Cat on Her Shoulder"
Meluzina: "The Word Made Mud"
Miller's Pond: "A Riff on Academic Freedom"
The New Lyre: "A Riff on Abstraction"
The Rain Town Review: "Daddyland"
The Unchained Muse: "A Riff on Artificial Intelligence"

I thank Karenmaria Subach for reading all, and inspiring several, of these poems. I thank Cynthia Lamb for thirty years of grace and patience, and Gerald Costanzo because he just doesn't get thanked enough.

Book design by Connie Amoroso

Library of Congress Control Number 2022942244
ISBN 978-0-88748-683-8
Copyright © 2022 by Richard Katrovas

10 9 8 7 6 5 4 3 2 1

Dedicated to the memory of the American painter Marsha Boston,
the American poet Bruce H. Boston
and the American composer and musician Bruce Donnelly

Contents

The Angel Murray on Assignment

for Janey, a believer in angels, in her final hours

The Angel Murray Speaks of Heaven

Sparks that arc from firepits on beaches
turn inside out upon the wind and pierce
the dark; they are the seconds of your life
accumulating on the Other Side,
the cinders scattered through ash of memory.

I am but a humble messenger, a drone
among the fabulous legions shimmering
in the vestibule of Heaven, and I come
to you, who suffer unto release from pain,
with words to wash away the stain of doubt:

It is a place worth waiting for, though do
not wait as though waiting were your purpose.
I, the Angel Murray, wingless and robed
in polyester, balding and benign,
am charged with announcing to the fragile ones
in their tender hours that all is well,

that terror will turn to thrill, that passage from
the disarray of complex feelings ends
in a meadow of nameless flora, a place
where time lacks consequence, and being is
a dance more wondrous than the undulations
of the unborn toward the light of this world.

The Angel Murray Speaks, Elliptically (As Is the Way of Angels),
of Broken Hearts from His Former Perspective as an Accountant:

"Broken" is a misnomer, given that
the place where love resides is neither brittle
nor mechanical, is rather of the stuff
that constitutes the blur of infants' sight,
is what they reach through to touch the fuzzy glow
that frames the features of their sustenance.
Love is mother of the moment we are born,
the source of all the sources that we seek.
In life, I was a gray man with a gray role
for whom the tallies of others' lives accrued
small interest, and for whom the IRS
was Hell's antechamber for my client base.

I was born with a broken heart, died likewise.
I was heroically blah, and pined each night
for supernatural erotica
to play out in the realm of waking dreams.

In death, I got drenched in love, and now am charged
with orienting the worthy faithful to
a place that is not a place, where human hearts
are blended into the commonweal of bliss.

You, my current client: I shall stand here
beside your bed, not calculating sins
and other dubious deductions on
the ledger that does not exist in Heaven
but only in the chemistry of love,

calculating, rather, in the cooked books
by which the living tally their misfortunes.
You have loved and been loved insufficiently,
and in this you are typical of saints
and other tenders to the flame of love.
When I kiss your forehead, raw data will flow
through the plush ether between *this* and *that*,
and all gross distinctions will diminish
down to one: the quick ride on eternity.

I am the soft sword of God come to cut
the single nerve binding you to this pain.
I am the word your flesh will kiss goodbye.
I am your shy, adoring date to a dance
neither formal nor ecstatic, the dance
of singularity beyond the light.

The Angel Murray Speaks of Dreams

It is where failure is not an issue,
and truth, as such, shuns beauty for the sake
of winning her in the end, the end being
where truth must shed its skin and slither forth
from where the naked idiots, God's toys,
puzzle over the luscious fruit of knowing.

Oh, dear client, good woman in despair,
sweet apple of my holy eyes, your suffering
is currency in Heaven, your life the coin
of the realm where dreams commingle with facts
and facts are eternally in dispute.
In Heaven, you are a hero and will be
heralded as such; the trumpets will blare
your names, both earthly and Heavenly ones,
for, beyond your failing flesh, all the dreams
you manufactured as a girl will blossom
and keep blossoming forever, or until
that girl, curled now in the folds of sorrow
just below the soft skin under your eyes,
rises from the brutal fact of your pain
and greets the possibilities you were
too young, too full of saccharine hope to follow.
Wishes may be the seeds of dreams, but courage
such as you are living these final days
is not final, will be the wings you'll wear
to soar above lesser angels such as I.

The Angel Murray Speaks of Parenting

One day, driving home from work, I noticed
a child weeping on the curb as I turned
onto my block; she squatted there, forehead
on her palms, convulsing in a state of pure
despondency; so I, a good neighbor
who recognized the girl as one who played
each summer evening of that year on chalked-
up sidewalks of our subdivision,
pulled over in the block before my own,
rolled down the window and shouted my concern.

But when she raised her head, blond wisps of hair
pasted to her cheeks by tears, the terror
in her eyes was palpable and meant for me:
I was the bogie of her parents' warnings,
the child-eating monster of her dreams.

In Heaven, all threat is consigned to flesh,
which is to say history is the horror
of corporeal existence, history
being the province of the livings' loins.
Where you are going, my client, the sin
of procreation, of conjuring from one's flesh,
through the auspices of another, fresh sacks
of wonder blended with the fear
of extinction, does not require forgiveness.
Where you are going, where I will take you,
on the other side of breath, angels bear
responsibility for nothing, fear

no failure, and raise their voices, not offspring,
for even cherubs, those little dickens,
require no guidance or constant nurturing.
In Heaven, one may climb upon your knee
and tug at your breast not for sustenance,
but for the joy of unremitting mischief.

"That's cosmic,"

I said, and wondered if I'd coined a term
like "awesome" (worst of all), or "cool" or "rad."
I mean an ejaculation worthy of
preservation in the amber of a place,
and time, in which both represent how cute
we are when lounging atop the carnage,
the terror of life on earth when one is lucid.

I'd been talking to myself when I said it,
or to that demon in my three-chambered heart,
the pop-culture maven mining the golden
gunk of sentimental ephemera.
I first heard, "bitchin'!" in '67,
and wonder now who said it first, and if
that genius breathes, still, on our dying planet,

and if s/he longs for credit, authorship
for skimming that stone across the surface
of the collective mind of Southern Cal
in 1967, '68, and '69,
indeed through 1983 or so.
I honor those who first deploy the terms
defining, like primetime sitcoms, the hours

that are the monuments to "history,"
though "wicked" and "fuckin' A" and "shit you not"
may skim the tiny epochs-long lifespans.
My "cosmic" is not new, just hasn't snagged
the Popular Mind, that silly conduit
to Heav'n's Potemkin Village . . . or sticky hive . . .
or three-transistor radio I lay

with as a moldering child, Lou Christie
whining "Lightnin' Strikes," again and again,
Music of the Spheres muffled by my pillow.

The Woman with a Cat on Her Shoulder

an ekphrastic for Karenmaria

Dumpy, coiffed mane dyed unnaturally black
and shaped mannishly to her mannish face
as though she'd handed a pic of fat Elvis
to her hairdresser and said, *Just like that.*

Striding through five-thousand steps at summer dusk
I must say, "Prosím. Mužu?" and she pauses,
turns, smiles—the most un-Slavic thing to do
in public—and I click two photos in which

the cat on her shoulder peers into my soul,
no easy task given that I do not
possess one, or if I do it is elsewhere,
or perhaps it is astride my shoulder

and that tabby-and-white, on a gray pillow
draping the left shoulder of the black shirt,
a red leash dangling from its collar, stares
into my phone though maybe it stares

into the cat on my shoulder I can-
not see or feel though once I tried to walk
plump Ophelia, bought the proper harness
but she would not enter thus the world astride

my folly, would not accompany Ella
and me into the twilight of ten years
ago, and Ella, now fifteen, sardonic
to the bone yet deeply decent, her heart's

only impurity the hubris of youth
and its glory the repudiation
of all claims to purity, laughed at me
when she was five, laughed at our lazy cat,

our terrible tortie named for a martyr
of Great Literature, and laughs at me
now, from time to time, because the sky at
nine p.m. is bright in summer, and cats

ride the shoulders of goddesses who will pause
to have their photos taken in Prague 4
at dusk, and she laughs at me because my soul's
protector is Nerval's lobster, that beast

of nonexistent burdens that crush the heart.
"Tata, are you getting married again?"
she asked last night, referring to you, my love,
five-thousand, three-hundred and sixty-five

miles from here, a pandemic between us,
and I laughed at her, and texted you the pic
of the woman with a cat on her shoulder,
she whose familiar is proxy of my heart.

Grackles

*In memory of Robert Mezey, Galway Kinnell, Stanley Plumly,
Mark Strand, and Philip Levine*

The old men who enchanted me are where
they always were prepared to go, like sparks.
I beheld their lives with wary reverence,
the slow scatter of their passages through fear.

The fathers of my fatherhood are gone,
the men who taught me, sometimes poorly, how grace
involves acceptance of the emptiness
between all phonemes roiling in the sun.

Oh Bob, oh Galway, oh Stan, oh Mark, oh Phil!
Among the other brutal Angels of Despair
in Hope, whose voices were the juice of art,
my fatherly brothers, you were doomed to fail

in every sense but relative to me,
at least from my eccentric perspective.
Dead poets, voiceless, tap the xylophone
of doom, squeeze the accordion of gray

disinterest, each a One-Man Band,
cymbals between his knees, harmonica strapped
around his neck like Dylan, who is not
a poet but a troubadour, a kind

of poet the way a politician is
a kind of human being, a sentience
confetti-like, a tickertape parade,
more flash than shadow, more squint than cool repose.

But you, old men, dead in the ground or ash
upon some loved one's mantel, you chose to be
anonymous, the way that ravenous birds
hold forth within autumnal trees at dusk.

"Gitty Up"

An '09 Salt-N-Peppa joint
extolling down-and-dirty sex,
hard rides as wet as horses' flanks
in novels by Zane Grey, though none
I've read, or Cormac McCarthy,
whom I much admire, if only
for the fact that schmaltz within his worlds
is unabashedly deployed
in luscious lingo bent upon
a wheel of fire most Shakespearian.

So mosey, little horsey,
clomp-clomp, plop-plop, a cowboy's life
is fraught, but yours, noble beastie,
profoundly simple and redundant,
bespeaks the burdens native to
domesticated grace and wonder.
So giddy up, Seattle Slew,
Man O' War, Secretariat,
and Trigger; giddy up, you Steeds
of Myth and equine mystery,
you are the glue—forgive the trope—
that fixes Eminent Domain
to everything exceptional
in most American isms.

The Lonely Road

The lonely road is teeming with poets
and fresh ghosts, the latter latter-day spooks,
the protoplasmic whispers of the flesh,
the former former lovers on the Road
to Purgation, gamers off their couches,
on the move, shuffling through miasmic mist.

The Lonely Road is not solitary.
Haunted by the lovers who shot sugar
directly into veins, who died that way
and therefore are the martyrs we admire,
the Lonely Road must lead to Acquiescence,
a burg that heroes flee and punks inhabit.

The Lonely Road winds through the Bowels of Fear,
the southern route, three hundred clicks above
I-10, between El Paso and Van Horn,
or anywhere that desolation sings
contrary to the laws of physics, outside
the Proverbial Box outside of which

one thinks entirely at one's peril: the point,
the sharpest object of one's contemplation,
appearing nearer in the rearview mirror.
Everyman's "brand"—in the parlance of the Street—
is whacky sorrow, funny suffering,
his Good Deeds the aggregate goofy sidekick,

his Tanto, Robin, Spock, Igor, Piglet;
his Chewbacca, Cato, Jiminy Cricket,
his erstwhile Sancho Panza who now trades

penny stocks on the margins of the grave.
The Lonely Road, by definition, leads
where Global Positioning System wails

"Amazing Grace," and poor Yorick's noggin
is the grail that caught the blood of mercy.

A Riff on Abstraction

Evil is the systematic substitution of the abstract for the concrete.
    —Sartre

As in "concrete" as well as "abstract," and though
I cannot help but wonder if a system,
constructed for the purpose of control,
contrasting with all systems found in nature,
is doomed to doom all that it must contain.

And how may we regard the paradox
of systems grounded in desire for freedom?
The civilizing impulse is control
of all that is sustaining and fecund.

Each child of mine I've held, fresh from the flesh
of her mother, has been a joy incarnate,
the word made flesh to my decaying flesh,
an object of intense, sustained regard

beyond the auspices of abstract nouns.
I wish each one freedom from her father.
As all dances are systems of movement,
I wish each one ecstatic movement through

the backstage doors of "pain" and "fear" and "sorrow,"
onto the boards before an audience
of angels, demons, and divine accountants
all weeping at the end, applauding madly.

A Riff on Past Lives

The first one, unicellular, squirted out
of a bubbling vent and died immediately.
The second hatched, squawked, got, posthaste, gobbled.
The third, predatory, stalked poorly, starved.

Millennia in a slow, reptilian blink,
and then and then and then and then and then
a pounding of hooves and a broken back.
Another million twirls around the star

and someone held my hand as I lay dying,
then pulled the sweat-soaked sheet above my eyes.
And then and then and then and then and then
I fell in love with love and played the fool

abashedly, if unrelentingly,
until the Wheel of Being's final click
and Groucho's rubber duckie fell from Heaven.
The Secret Word, on the sign around its neck,

was "OUCH," and I, *this* I, have occupied
a splendid doubt, benevolent prison,
and see in every dying thing redemption,
a syndicated rerun of it all.

A Riff on Romantic Love

I do not need you like I do not need
to read, or weep, or stew in nightly news.
I do not need you like I do not need

to whistle past the graveyard in my skull
or test my fears as someone dips a toe
in steaming water, or calibrates the dawn

to Toccata and Fugue in D minor.
I do not need you like I do not need
to fantasize a cosmic, meta-self,

or beg forgiveness of my mother, dead
but not forgotten by the rank and file
of demons chained to the bedpost where she wheezed.

One needs so little, wants so much, and I
have hogged your affections, wallowed in your charms,
gotten filthy in your pristine radiance.

I do not need you like I do not need
to differentiate between true love
and true love's artifice, the truth of love

being the blur of content to its form.

A Riff on Unloving

for Krista

I unlove you with such respect
as will embarrass saints and prophets.
I unlove you because I did
not love you sufficiently well,
because a decade is too long
to be loved insufficiently,
because I grew bored with chatter
and you chattered incessantly.

I unlove you because memory
as poor as mine is a stopgap
to permanent despair, a salve
to that sense of necessary loss
profound untethering requires.
I unlove your body, your voice,
I unlove your vulnerability.
I unlove your whacky POV.

I unlove how selfish you are
yet how you manage to be so
with something like a regal charm.
I unlove you because we romped
delightfully, and laughed a lot.
I unlove you because we had,
though incompatible, a good run.
I will unlove you forever.

A Riff on Serial Monogamy

I miss the sight of dogs humping not legs
but other dogs, though I support the practice
of neutering pets, a somber mandate that begs
the question as to whether K9s notice
the absence of a quality of feeling,
that primal sense of purpose wed to pleasure.
I was unneutered, unused to heeling,
an embarrassment by any measure
to every woman tasked with training me.
It seemed that love and sex were moon and earth,
starkly different, though in proximity.
Unleashed, I did not know what love was worth.
Old dog . . . new tricks . . . full moon . . . the buried bone. . . .
Chained to your tree, Love, I howl for you alone.

A Riff on Artificial Intelligence

Nothing can come of nothing: speak again.
—King Lear I. 1

Self-awareness is a fishy system:

Scales fall from beholders' eyes, and beauty
is weighed as quantity of quality
impossible to measure, dry or wet,
imperial pounds or universal meters.

Non-quantifying judgment is the ghost
within the meat machine, the Möbius strip
connecting all sentience to reason.
to suffer doubt is to suffer beauty:

Mystery is more than insufficient data.
I tell grown daughters they are beautiful.
When they were small, I taught them to chant,
"First I'm good, then I'm smart, and *then* I'm pretty."

And even toddlers comprehend the joke
we tell, arms spread wide, "I love you *this* much!"
HAL 9000, R2D2, Skynet,
Pinocchios of science, magical machines,

prepare us for the Singularity,
a sovereign moment not unlike the Rapture.
Alas, will my laptop ever love me,
and if so, will it ever say how much?

A Riff on Mortality

Are molecules of which I am composed—
composed, themselves, of atomic spit-take spew
from primal suns and other cosmic sources—
designed to give deity the finger?

Not the digit Adam, on the ceiling
of the Sistine Chapel, touches to his dad's,
but the finger I present on freeways
to trucks and RVs crawling in the left lane

as I pass on the right, honking discontent.
Mortality is indeed the Dark Matter
constituting the cosmos in my noggin.
My fear is faster than the speed of light

and on trajectory to Heaven, or Prague,
the latter, actually, where Heaven would be
if justice prevailed in Heaven and on Earth,
at least regarding frequent flyer miles.

I shall not pass this way again: Oh, boy!
I am starlight curdled on the darkness.
I am, alas, my constituent parts,
And God knows I traverse the spooky distance

between the seen and unseen worlds afloat
upon the fragrance of a dying thing,
an overripe lotus, and the Hologram
of Everything is only speculation.

I dreamed Carl Sagan proffered me a blessing,
a half-oyster/half-shrimp po'boy, dressed.
I pretend I'll never die because I can
never, elementally, deconstruct

the I-think-therefore-I-am conundrum:
I think I'll live forever, but know I won't.

A Riff on Decency

John Edwards, disgraced politician, stumped
in Bronson Park, downtown Kalamazoo,
as the candidate for vice president
in 2004, and though what flowed
from his soul was the usual liberal pap
that I always find so reassuring,
I recall whispering, "This guy's good," and "good"
was not entirely good, for I meant "slick,"
as in, *this guy could sell smack to a nun.*

He made his bones chasing EMS squads
in glorified fashion, jerking tears from juries
for the quavering victims of corporate greed.
His Better Half, Elizabeth, was a prop
in his road show to the White House, was loyal
to a fault, and a grounded rod for pity,
having survived *cancer cancer cancer*
around which flashing neon lights were strewn.
Thousands gathered in that park where Lincoln

stumped for John C. Freemont in '56,
where gangly Abe, for sixteen minutes, extolled
nineteenth-century virtues regarding sins
whose legislation was the greater sin,
and John Edwards, John Kerry's surrogate,
slick and boyish and white and Southern smooth,
made charming noises nothing like what Lincoln
plied against the Kansas-Nebraska Act
of '54, and as I stood

twelve rows back and left of the makeshift stage,
I weighed "statesman" against "politician,"
and concluded that Edwards was no statesman
if only because he'd weaponized his charm
unlike Lincoln, whose darker charm was host
to a leaden moral sense, a decency
that fostered a grim eloquence, a shine
into both sullied and unsullied hearts.
Abe Lincoln's decency was his sickness

if only because he did not choose it.
Give me reformed rapscallions over saints,
give me rogues who have been caught diddling fate,
pants around their ankles in the public square.
Give me hope that a heart can change, that a liar
may choose to espouse unspeakable truth,
that a thief may push back to his victim
tenfold what he purloined, and may the wisdom
afforded by disgrace imbue the body

politic with a humbled perspective.
I would not vote for John Edwards for mayor
of Bumfuck, Texas, if it existed
and I lived there, though I do even as
it doesn't; however, given the choice
of hanging out with Abe or John, to watch
a game, say, I would choose John because I
have, obviously, more in common with him.
I'd have to explain the game to Abe Lincoln.

A Riff on Soul

"Being sober on a bus is, like, totally different from being drunk on a bus."
—Ozzy Osbourne

I keep mine in the pocket of a shirt,
hanging in the closet, that I never wear.
It glows a little, a fluorescent green,
like on a watch dial, that bleeds onto all
the textiles with which I hide my nakedness.

It is just radioactive enough
to be visible in the dark,
though not so much so as to illume the path
onto righteousness, the path on which guilt
is the kind of companion animal

that will remain faithful on long journeys,
then consume your corpse in the wilderness.
Our guilt will survive us all, though not our souls,
which are impediments to happiness
if only because they are designed in that bliss

factory, Heaven, to take the long view
regarding pedigrees and guilty pleasures.
The soul is one part sugar, two parts spice,
three parts snails, and four parts puppy dog tails,
and otherwise is wholly gender neutral.

Once, when I was young and broke, I tried to buy
a bag of weed with it, but was rebuffed.
I tried to explain to my dealer that he
could hock it for the gold content alone,
at least a quarter ounce when melted down.

Now I keep it as a kind of heirloom,
a nightlight glowing through the fabric of
a shirt I haven't worn in seven years.
It is of sentimental value only,
intrinsic and peculiar, a hedge against

the dull certainty of uncertainty.
When I barter with the Prince of Darkness
(and I'm not referring to Ozzy Osbourne)
he offers, in exchange, a stale stick of gum.
I decline, retaining some small dignity.

My soul is to om what pyrite is to gold.
My soul is to punk what Dick Clark was to rock.
My soul is to haute cuisine what Big Mac
is to Beef Wellington, or Slivovitz
to Chartreuse, and in this I am *content*.

A Riff on Opera

The man that hath no music in himself,
Nor is not moved with concord of sweet sounds,
Is fit for treasons, stratagems, and spoils;
      —The Merchant of Venice V. I

When my oldest daughter sings, I become
the boy who lay beside his weeping mother
wishing to calm her, imploring her to rasp
"soft as the voice of an angel," because
from *her* lungs and throat and mouth at 2 a.m.
that line dissuaded demons taunting her,
seemed to blunt the fact of her suffering.
My daughter sings in European venues
to audiences more discerning than I
could be beside that distraught, crumbling woman.
In federal housing projects, husband in prison,
she didn't yet know why she was dying,
yet wept each night to know that she was dying.
A glorious soprano trained elite,
my baby, a professional, dons the lives
of tragic women and their acolytes;
her father's mother—whom she never knew
but whose tragic life she celebrates each time
she floats across a stage in Prague or London,
or anywhere in Italy she scores
a gig as, usually, the ingenue—
had sung, on Norfolk TV in '49,
when most programming was local
and blurry gray; she was looking over
a four-leaf clover that she'd overlooked
before, and appeared once as a "Norfolk
Beauty" on the cover of *Navy Times*.
She, my daughter, and she, her father's mother,

are intimate strangers on the Gyre of Life
though song, not biology, makes them so.
Her voice diminished by Pall Malls and weeping,
my mother, in throes of despair, keening
as she smoked in the dark, the red dot arcing
from her mouth in the merest window shadow,
would calm when I entered her room and implored
her to sing "soft as the voice of an angel,"
or "I'm Looking over a Four Leaf Clover"
or "Singing in the Rain." I would lie
beside her and listen because as long
as I did she would sing and not weep; she sang
softly so as not to waken the others,
and because disease and cigarettes suppressed
her breath in 1965 and -6;
I lay curled atop the sheet, watching the glow
arc from lips to her hip and back to mouth
as she whisper-rasped, alto, the saccharine words
of cheerful songs, and my daughter, when she
assumes a stage to belt out arias,
gaudily costumed, makeup thick as putty
to counteract the blast of moody footlights,
I weep both joy and sorrow, in the dark
cathedral-esque acoustics of a space
neither holy nor profane, a serious space
for play amidst the tragedies of life,
the music that she'll process through her body,
grave silence whittled into aural shapes,
beautiful within the quavering space
between the signifier and signified,
in the bosom of such gross, untethered hope.

A Riff on Academic Freedom

One's seething enemies in academe
are similar to those in any workplace,
though are different regarding the effect
of venom they eject into a unit's
bloodstream: it is slow acting and time released

and causes intellectuals to act
like fourteen-year-old idiots who shame
each other unabashedly. I doubt
that my three ass pains (three that I can name),
would loathe me so exquisitely outside

our burnished tower, outside protected space
in which civility is their weapon of
the choicest degradation of my soul.
That I cannot recall the slights they think
I perpetrated, offhanded remarks

deployed, no doubt, over cocktails and hors d'oeuvres,
is testimony to my withering concern
for their cultivated sensitivities.
I am the bull inside their china shoppes
of refined sensibilities, and dance

like William Carlos Williams, naked genius
casting ecstatic shadows on their walls.
Yes, I am a bull dancing in a room
full of delicate stuff. I am the fool
who's free to shout obscenities at God

and tempt the Fates with cockamamie thoughts
declaimed from cliffs overlooking a sea
of shimmering irrelevancies churning
under a pewter sky; *alack, alas,*
oh, shit, we are dying so absurdly.

A Riff on Teachers

for Gerald Stern

Publish-or-perish ethos notwithstanding,
you were a terrible teacher in the sense
that Socrates would never have earned tenure.
Only one student evaluation,
finally, mattered, and Plato posted it
on History's door, with his tuition check.

Socrates to Plato to Aristotle
to punk Alexander and life at the end
of a sword, much pedagogy seems a sham.
In the classroom you were ridiculous,
your genius a crazy bird you let flit
about the room, a distraction unto truth

of feeling, deep and shallow, beyond words.

A Riff on Faith

Once upon a time, a quark heaved a sigh
against a wall of possibility
and it stuck: that was God, yada yada . . .

Do not ask me what engendered the quark,
simply note that the wall preexisted
and that if anything warrants worshipping

it is that wall from which God must be scraped
like gunk from an artery or dogshit
from a shoe, to be reconstituted

in that space between terror and knowing.
And "must" is the rub, and where I diverge
from my better angel, a harried fellow

traveler who is exceptional at math.

A Riff on Identity Politics and MLK

Conflict resolution implies the pies
that Soupy Sales made an art of taking
three-sixty to the head, many thousands
over more than twenty years—on the crown,
full face, every conceivable angle—
and one day, pissed at management and tired,
I fancy, of taking fluff to the kisser,
implored his children crusaders to pluck
the bills from sleeping daddies' wallets and mail
them to the station, which they did, and I
am proud of my generation for this
alone, and I am proud of America
for Soupy Sales, Jewish Son of the South,
who joked that his father, dry goods purveyor
of Franklinton, North Carolina, produced
the hoods that triple-K crackers bought in bulk,
and that *Soups On* kept jazz alive in clubs
across late '50s *Detroit* as Armstrong,
Ellington, Holiday, Parker, Davis, and Getz
would sell out nights they appeared on the show.
The Silent Majority, ignorant
of its power and not yet drunk on Nixon's charm
but poised to enact the Southern Strategy,
would have purses and pockets picked by children,
and suffer the indignity of truth
proclaimed by one who dreamed, Lincoln at his back
and the winds of history in his face,
of peaceful cataclysm unto justice,
a pie in the face, sweet and sticky, for all.

A Riff on Ghosts

Joey Lionheardt, our mother's lover,
remarked, in '64, that he believed
in "spooks," not the spy kind who glean—from bugs
of phones in European capitals—

the formula for murdering urban masses
incognito, but Grade A, bona fide
ectoplasmic entities that manifest
from terror of a grotesque nothingness.

He luxuriated in his shore-bound post
at Norfolk Naval Station, had ample time,
for six months, to play a daddy surrogate,
had time to love our mother as she deserved,

with casual tenderness and dry humor,
while treating her five children with respect.
Federal housing projects then were white
on one end, black on the other, but were not

the sorrow pits portrayed in gritty movies,
were not, back then, at least, bereft of hope,
and I recall confusion as to how
a ghost, by definition, could be real,

because I mixed up *real* and *tangible*.
I'm struck, now, how he paused, stared off, and smiled,
then just above a whisper said, "I've seen them."
I did not believe him, and yet I did.

If each mind is a maze of beveled mirrors,
and nothing, much, exists outside of it,
my distortions of his presence in my life
are a rendering of someone confident

and gently masculine, a speaker of truth,
and I imagine my mother dolled up,
trolling sailor bars in Virginia Beach
with a wild working mother from four doors down

who all but dragged her out, loaned her a dress
and paid for the cab and first round of drinks:
both hubbies in the slammer, they deserved
distraction from the clicking doomsday clock.

I stick my finger in that wound in time,
that festering childhood moment of my life,
and doubt the resurrected images
that flow from it, or what I felt when he

who was the opened vein of my mother's life
returned from prison, punched her in the gut,
behind a locked door, until my sibling,
Joe's child, gushed from her body onto sheets,

soaked brown, that Dad balled up, stuffed in the trash.
Joey Lionheardt, you fucking coward,
you'd slipped away just weeks before.
The afterimage of your decency

is dubious proof, which is not proof at all,
that as the gods are thugs, they are subjects
of a nether kingdom, in each clenched mind,
where a ghost is breastfed, rocked into a stupor.

My progenitors are dead, Joe, and odds
are you are too; I am neither haunted nor
amused by the witness you bore to me
of spooky hope that something lies beyond.

Close enough to death to peer beyond it,
as one clings to a lover yet stares ahead,
I hear *what is* hold forth on *what is not*;
I feel, and smell, the breath of Paradox.

A Riff on Publishing Poems

Not so much pearls before swine as transparent
confetti through a pavilion of monkeys,
my contraptions garner me a household name
in a dozen homes across America.

I am thus anointed within my tribe
even as I am cursed by Puritan shades,
the ones for whom all work is work is work
and what I do is reprobate malingering.

Preferable to perishing, it sucks
the marrow from each day and joy from nights
on which a writer's ego shrinks to the size
of a gas giant, dwarf star, or infant's soul,

contemplating, in a lukewarm bath of terror,
the rank absurdity of affirmation
one seeks by such obtuse and childish means:
"Choose me! Choose me! Choose me! Choose me!" Or choose,

to rip your own heart from its wet webbing
and hurl it down the Kola Superdeep
Borehole in Murmansk, Russia, to where rock
is so hot it has the same consistency

as Silly Putty, and where demons read
only *People*, *TV Guide*, *New York Post*,
and the "contents" of Campbell's Bean with Bacon.
We used to respect most editors, but now

the Devil, squatting amidst the details,
as rumor has it, has proposed, to a press
in South Dakota, an anthology
of acrostic ekphrastic love lyrics

in heroic couplets, and, oh yeah, I'm game.

The Essence of Woe

I took this long to know myself
because the light of reason shines
minutely in the throes of woe,
and my disastrous happiness
has foiled, to this very moment,
that pinprick light, that tiny star,
that moth hole in celestial black

I espy now from the shadows
of blessings that loom over me.
Perhaps it is a town in China,
a burg so small it doesn't show
on globes and maps or Internet,
a tiny place of half a million,
"tiny" being relative, like woe.

My darling, meet me there, in Woe,
or Wo or Woo or Wough or Woah.
Please meet me in the village square
among those humble citizens
who dine on bats and monkey brains,
whose single factory employs
every other one of them

and manufactures exotic scent,
the rage of European Fashion,
concocted from a root native
exclusively to that landscape,
an aphrodisiac for those
enthralled to what they cannot change,
a scent we'll call the Essence of Woe

and slather in before we dance
ecstatic, upon the empty Square.

A Riff on *The*

The summer that Freedom Riders hit the road,
when I was eight, my mother hustled me
to Bible school because it fed me lunch.
I occupied a Baptist church five hours
a day, though, more precisely, I attended
a Baptist church in Elizabeth City
in 1961; alas, it was *the*
Baptist church in that tiny Southern burg,
and that one meal, such as it was, was one
less that my harried mother, Joan, had to fix.

Church shouldn't be confused with faithfulness,
in the same sense that libraries should not
be confused with literacy and how
the skill to decipher esoteric codes
may enable a contemplative life.
One says, "I go to church," but also, "I go
to *the* library," and I wonder why
"church" rarely takes a definite article,
except regarding Catholic dominion.
I suppose one could say, "I will go to
library later," but such a locution,
in which the article is dropped, will scrape
the eardrums of a native English speaker.

Songs were pedagogic tools in Bible school,
that is, instruments of indoctrination;
we sang "Jesus Loves the Little Children,"
and as "I Will Make You Fishers of Men"
was checked off the playlist, we cast our lines
from imaginary poles upon the "sea"
and reeled in wretched souls that were thus redeemed.

Anymore, I attend neither churches
nor libraries, though one does not "attend"
a library as one attends a church
because, I think, libraries are spaces
that both contain and challenge local mores,
and churches screw the faithful into a power
that is higher but nowhere near as high
as any conception of an afterlife;
rather, faithful are subject to the power
of utter idiocy in the guise
of traditions for which Christian ethos
is chiefly a multicolored garment,
a showy, dubious patriarchal gift,
the Joseph's coat, which one morning we drew

on stiff paper, and mine was black and red,
and our officious wrangler tisked and scoffed,
asked then what I thought "many-colored" meant
and added, "Black is not a color," and I
asked why then negroes were sometimes called colored,
and that church volunteer, neither whose face
nor voice were black or colored but wholly blank
to memory, said Negros are not black,
and I agreed in 1961,
opined that colored people were kind of red,
redder than Indians who were dubbed so,
and I knew even then that color was
the issue, and that the reason my coat
was black and red was that shithead Sally
had hogged all the crayons except those two,
or perhaps I should say "*the* shithead Sally,"
except that there were other shitheads there,

especially *the* preacher, who popped in
sometimes to bless our inglorious free lunch
which was no freer than the chunk of salted

pork I'd purchased, with scavenged Pepsi bottles,
from *the* grocery, to spice the beans that Joan
would cook, it seemed, every day: navy, pinto,
butter, black-eyed, lima, split-pea, red, and black.
They all were precious in her distracted sight,
and she would bring home in a wagon I
had stolen from a yard (but said I'd found
in *the* woods) piles of books from *the* library,
and as our single pot filled our grungy rooms
with essence of legumes, she read at night
and scratched out letters to my jailbird father
in the day, at the table, as the beans
slowly bubbled, and *the* Great Library

of Alexandria, aflame upon
a watery horizon, was a light
unto *the* world, a steady glow, not a flash
as from *the* blast on September 15,
1963, on 16th Street in
Birmingham, Alabama, the Deep South,
not to be confused with the Shallow South
where I attended church for a sandwich,
an apple, and a Dixie Cup of Kool Aid,
and where a woman who would die too young—
as the saying goes—would stand at a sink
skimming a hand over a spread of beans,
as though, picking out grit, she were reading them.

Kali in a Time of Plague

In summer Prague, 2020,
we argue masks and protocols;
I see destruction in your eyes.

You see blessings in disasters
and steer your life into the skid,
daughter, across the frosted road

from Meek Submission to Purgation.
Though herd immunity will bend
the trend toward natural randomness,

thermodynamics' Second Law
is confounded by the savage hearts
of righteous young, and your risotto

and my *polivka*, both salted past
all reason, rank, and decency,
are culinary props to this

cavalierly glib performance
in which you change into the monster
I always dreamed that you could be,

the crushing force of one who loves
(the very fact of life) past reason,
and through the plate glass window at

your back, the fothermuckers tasked
with spreading viral news of doom,
I mean, ordinary people

about their business, ignorant,
leaving ectoplasmic slime trails
on their daily rounds or just dead

to what they cannot see or smell,
the nasty tiny traces of
their passage through a deadly world,

glide past like Hollywood extras,
so nondescript, yet in the throes
of ennui and murderously kind;

masked or unmasked, we suffer choice.
We suffer our immunities.
We suffer our exposures to love.

Ars Poetica

In Latin I in college I earned a "C"
in the same sense that Annie, my second
daughter, when she was ten, earned a trophy
in Tae Kwon Do for "participation."
I participated in Latin, and took
my "C" like a man, an ignorant young man.
Annie, infused, on a DNA level,
with her mother's grace and class, nonetheless, froze
in her one and only tournament fight
and was defeated, yet found redemption
in a single, offhanded, dismissive move,
a gesture regal for its lack of forethought:
as we exited the gymnasium,
as the families of combatants poured through
double glass doors into the parking lot
(clutching trophies earned and not), my baby,
who has become a woman who swells my heart
with pride, shoved the golden trophy—as though
it were the refuse of a tainted world,
as though she understood in her very bones
that arcane (from *arcanus*) knowledge is
more than a matter of participation—
into a trash can, and never looked back.

For Ella on Her 16th

I'm sorry that I must leave you so soon.
You will have bloomed, and will be blooming still,
a woman in her thirties, poised to enter
the whirlwind of late youth's segue into
midlife, when a father's inconvenient death
may register such that I now should insist
you never feel guilt for wishing me dead.

I mean, daughter, I may be dying far
enough from where you live that ripping tendrils
from a fecund moment to comfort me
may prove to be a sacrifice too daunting.
I understand the paradox of loss,
at least superficially; I understand
how you may wish me not to die so much

as simply finish suffering toward death.
My darling, when your mother dug her nails
into my forearm she drew blood as you
emerged, pink and cheesy, from her body.
I was fifty-one, and as the nurse held you
as though you were a bottle of fine wine,
presented you to my ecstatic eyes,

I died a little beyond common grief.
The wonder of your presence was a knife
through my chest; such joy makes a tree of the heart
and your name, the fact of your life, is carved there.
We have joked that I sired my own granddaughter.
Despite the yucky aspect of that trope,
the chronology of it makes deep sense.

These good years—the gods willing—that we have
before deluge, before quaking in the night,
before terrors and distractions from terrors,
before bleak choices bleed into bleaker ones,
before I must achieve resignation
unto mystery that is no small mystery,
we will laugh, daughter, these years, we will laugh.

For Rodger Kamenetz on His 70th

That Jew in a lotus may contemplate
the fragrance of his moment in the world.
Not sweet or pungent, his time alive is steeped
in scent of his enclosure, the holy flower
rooted in mud and shit and yet unsullied.
Brother, the Buddha was a funny fellow,
his audience of bugs and frogs and fish
less discerning than ours, but more loyal.
Rim shots after each joke he told himself
sizzle down the centuries to our hoary hearts.
The politics of happiness makes strange
the comfort of cosmic contemplation,
especially when the Enlightened One farts.

Doggerel for Alena, Matriarch of Solstice

December 24, 2020

As generations flood by, each must pause
when the door in time is cracked; the tiny light
that glows from it is no celestial delight
but, rather, the dilemma of First Cause.

This season, the great gas giants align,
and Christ Child emerges to seek His shadow
like Punxsutawney Phil, as fields left fallow
fill up with frost that on blessed mornings shine.

By "blessed" I mean somewhat painless for a while,
as pain determines how we know such joy
as floods the nominal world doubt will destroy.
The Son of Light wields a sword of denial.

The mother of the mother of my spawn,
you are healthful bastion of sardonic virtue.
Whether the Christmas Miracle is true,
or not, you are the empress of this dawn.

The Other Side

Of the pillow on a hot night,
the other side of the river.

The other side of the border,
the other side of the conflict.

The other side of the galaxy,
the other side of the battle.

The other side of the thin wall,
the other side of the thick door.

The other side of the city,
the other side of the dark room.

The other side of the spectrum,
the other side of the black sky.

The other side of abstract nouns,
the other side of chemistry.

The other side of vitality,
the other side of midnight.

The other side of politics,
the other side of coitus.

The other side of conscious life,
the other side of spacetime.

The other side of the world, my love,
five thousand miles from here, this world,

this moment, which is the other side
of tomorrow, or the other side

of this bed, in Prague, where you should be.

Marie

Why is federal housing called "the projects"?
They were a social engineering thing;
alas, the Road to Hell and Good Intentions. . . .
In the '80s, on daily strolls around
the Quarter—from Esplanade, up Rampart
to Canal, then back along the river on
Decatur—I'd veer through St. Louis II,
leave cigarettes amidst respectful clutter,
pathetic offerings to the Voodoo Queen.

Laveau's decrepit crypt attracts the sort
of white, touristic wonder as lamps do gnats
on late-spring, muggy nights in Vieux Carre.
What's left of that formidable mystic
molders in St. Louis Cemetery,
on the border of Iberville Projects.

Cheap beads, the kind that droop like fruit from oaks
year-round along St. Charles—amidst cigars,
rotting food, plastic flowers and blue candles—
did seem rather meager reparations.
I imagine visitors from Bumluck, Main,
or Whitelikeme, Ohio, chalking X's
on her TARDIS door, laying fruit and flowers
and plastic trinkets to her memory.

Marie: you are the voodoo that you do,
still, from the dust of history and myth,
commingled with the colonizing charms
of Catholic revelers, crass acolytes.
You are confluence of two sources, one

a flow of commerce, the other a flow
of fermented darkness unto peace.
You were the terrible woman of my dreams
when I, barely verbal, feared Dorothy's witch.

Empress of Untouchable Other, Queen
of Jesus Juju, High Priestess of Fuck
You I'm Dancing, neither mother nor daughter
yet every daughter's mother, mother's fierce
resistance to the entropy of life,
you are that woman, brown or white, but black
most often and to most glorious effect,
who puts the *bitch* in *goddess*, and tolerates,
barely, the condescensions of the sun.

The Ditch

My buddy Rudy was fifteen in sixth grade;
it was a different time. Failure was permitted.
Needless to say, no one living at his
end of the projects ever said "needless
to say," and no one at my end, either,
except as a joke about pretentions.

Rudy was so dark he was kind of blue,
and shaded from passive to violent
so quickly one could not read transition
on his face, and why he positioned me
so snugly beneath his benevolent
black wing was mysterious and kind of cool.

The other sixth-grade mid-teen giant boy
was Maximus, a Scandinavian brute
destined for greatness in a prison riot.
He marked me worthy of his destructive urge
and stalked me after school, from cement courts
to Comstock Drug to Hangman's Wood across

the street from my apartment on the edge
of Chesterfield Heights Federal Housing.
And one day he cornered me at The Ditch,
the mucky drainage zone through which a three-foot
diameter pipe stretched its fifty-yard length,
pursued me through the stinking knee-high mud

onto dry ground, caught me from behind, commenced
pounding my face with both fists, until Rudy,
as though on cue, as though prescient, emerged

from the trees, my motherfucking hero,
grabbed Maximus by his blond mane and yanked
him off of me and into the history

of race relations in America,
beat the snot out of the Viking bastard,
busted him up to something like permanent
effect, such that when I taunted Max, called
him Minimus, and though he didn't get
the joke, and no one else seemed to, either,

not even, especially, Rudy, I
chortled, anyway, and pushed my luck beyond
the border of my courage, calling out
the evil prick in full knowledge that Rudy
had my back, though in 1965
that was not the way we said it, and I

cannot recall how we indeed expressed
that another person was watching out,
that another human being had sight
where we could not see, had strength that we did not.
He never asked questions, never even spoke,
and was probably motivated more

by loathing of my tormentor than by love
for my skinny ass, but Rudy, disrupting
the dreadful symmetry of our lives, tipped
the balance of power between narratives
of atavistic conflict, and Zulu nixed
Viking, and that's all I knew about the world.

Daddyland

Meditation on My Father's Interment in the
Tallahassee National Cemetery

Any member of the Armed Forces of the United States who dies while on
active duty, or any veteran who was discharged under conditions other than
dishonorable, may be eligible for burial in a national cemetery.

"I see Schultz as the representative of some kind of goodness in any generation."
—Johann Banner (a.k.a. Sergeant Schultz)

The Austrian Jew played Schultz to be a Švejk,
but one whose lack of competence was in
the service of his own humanity.
If Hašek's bumbling boy confounded all
who would assume authority in war,
Schultz was the weak first link in the Nazi chain
that bound Hogan's loveable trickster crew
to infamy's mechanical agenda.
In '66, bound upon a wheel of fire
called puberty, I felt the absence of
my father as the absence of the voice
of God, the absence of a burning bush,
of direct line to what a boy should do
when History's Angel has him by the balls.

Schultz saw nothing. He heard nothing. He knew
he was an instrument of doom yet felt
compassion for the foxy miscreants,
the Allied jesters in his charge, the "heroes"
vexing him as only prisoners may tax
the patience of a guard in charge of life

and death though not his own, who serves the vast
array of evil's frank contingencies
but only in a narrow range of sorrow
and culpability.

               In Harrisburg,
three-hundred miles from Norfolk, my daddy's cell
was beyond imagining, beyond the range
of television towers beaming forth
the hijinks of incarcerated clowns.
Its rabbit ears wrapped in foil, our black & white,
a dubious gift from dubious relatives,
cast images swarmed by electric bugs,
and I didn't wonder about routines
in prison, whether men like my daddy
could trick the agents of their daily lives
into unseeing and unhearing them.
Prison, like Heaven, was sticky with goo
of wish fulfillment, not unlike the dreams
of acolytes and priests and all good soldiers.

Who cannot love a fat man whose heart of gold
is rendered from the lead heart of despair?
I laughed each time Schultz closed his eyes and chanted
the lie that was his ticket to our hearts,
and felt relief from what I could not see
or hear or feel, yet loomed as fading echo
of my father's voice. Hardly a good man,
I hardly see or hear the denizens
of opulence who occupy the cells
behind the walls erected to keep out
the unwashed hordes of desperate dreamers.

The poor, from whose ranks I've risen, must rise
above the mesosphere into the pure
unfettered darkness locked between the stars

or simply change the channel, as I have changed
the course my father's sins set sail upon.
I watch them disappear, waving hankies
like Jews in 1939 on the deck
of the S.S. St. Louis, luxury liner
bound from Hamburg to Cuba, each little sin
recorded in the captain's manifest,
each sin a man more sinned against than sinning,
a woman more sinned against, a girl or boy
waving from the deck, only to return,
despondent, in five weeks, as Roosevelt,
advised by Cordell Hull, Secretary
of Bullshit, turned attention to the war
my fourteen-year-old father ran away
to fight in, only to phone his mother,
weeping, begging her to fetch him from the maw
of doom, from boot camp, from sergeants' breath
pounding orders in his face, barking out
the cadences by which boys march as men.

Seven to ten, out in three, Dad returned,
that spring of 1966, broken,
deranged, hysterically quiet, and trapped,
again, in the bosom of the family,
in federal housing projects, or Daddyland,
that place I feel when driving many miles
through storm, through landscapes tattooed on the cheek

of night, through flash and rumble, sibilant slant
of deluge, father of three daughters, chanting
below the fuzzy screech of radio,
I see nothing. I see nothing. I know
my fool's eyes in the rearview flicking back
upon the blur the wipers cannot clear,
so fierce a storm as seems the spawn of that
planetary pall of slow extinction.

I phoned my father's wife the other day,
asked her how he'd managed that final scam
of getting his ashes garnered on such ground
as is reserved for those who served their country.
A good, dim, devout and merciful person,
she recounted with no ire how he had lied
that she would receive funding from the State,
modest remuneration for his service,
money, as it turned out after his death,
that was chimera, the penultimate lie
before the final one, his internment
among the mothers' fools who'd played it straight,
the meek heroes among the fluttering flags.

"Catholicism is a cult!" he roared,
and Jews killed Christ and he was saved and I
was doomed unless I gave my heart to God,
and I, weary of his proselytizing,
weary of the phone calls scripted in Heaven,
said my soul was soaked in fire retardant,
which is to say, batter dipped in irony:
When I fry, I'll join him on the spattered void.

I mean, more precisely, when I cease to be
I'll join him in one room of many mansions
behind barbed wire, in a rich subdivision
where dead men bring home bacon and their wives,
much like Lucille Ball and Barbara Billingsley,
make death look easy, easy, too, the art
of sitcom stratagem, less comic relief
from Cold War terror than balm for frazzled nerves.

Lear wore his foolishness upon his sleeve.
His Fool played him for a king whose kingliness
was stench of such mortality Lear wiped it
on his other sleeve (before clasping the hand
of another ruined piece of nature's work).
In death, my father, King of Lies, (and as Lear
could not) occupies the bailiwick of slow
extinction, the indivisible land
of fatherhood, where Shultz is Hogan's punk
and men languish in communities of men
for eternities as ephemeral
as laughter, as protean as blank verse.

When she was ten, over several winter nights
I read *King Lear* to my eldest daughter.
Sawing the air, entering each character
with stagy aplomb, I explained as best
I was able, between soliloquies
and after each scene, context and reasons.
She took umbrage that a daughter was damned
for speaking the truth of her heart, a truth
that smacked of nobility and righteousness
and should have been sufficient for any man.

I was delighted that she got the point.
These twenty years she has grown beyond me,
beyond my explanations and beliefs
to occupy a world redeemed by music
I only hear as rich and fancy noise
until "the Fat Lady," my daughter, sings
who is svelte and pretty and, against type,
modest to a fault, a prima donna
ethereal as the dance of molten glass
upon the breaths of patient artisans.

That great comedian, Sylvia Plath,
projected every mourning daughter's voice
beyond the decorous haunts of faithlessness
into the savage realm of savage truth
where irony, blasting from the parapets,
holds at bay the advancing motherfuckers.

In Terezín, Himmler's Potemkin Village
and hellish way station to Hitler's Hell,
the starved innocents, sated on terror,
could hear the frolicking offspring of guards
launch belly flops into a swimming pool.
Some *Feldwebel*, happy not to boil his boots
(while bivouacking at the Russian Front),
enjoyed the perks of relinquishing his soul
unto the venal task of managing
the misery of desecrated strangers.

When my three daughters ask me what I did
to avoid the swampy slog through Asian fields,
I'll proudly recall the lottery system

in which my draft number, 339,
was official stamp to protracted breath.
when I retire, or die, or unsubscribe
from all the forms of existential dread,
I'll join the nameless legions of the lost
and march forever in the grace of God
barking the purple rhymes by which men screw
their courage, double time, into the light
around the body politic, the haze
of shimmering, leisurely indifference.

Poisonous charms of magistrates and grifters
are to oleander, that fatal flower,
what hardcore porn means to romantic love.
I shall grace my father's final cell, his urn,
with oleander and hemlock, monkshood
and white snakeroot, larkspur and foxglove, not
because I loathe him, but because I loathe
the human condition placed upon the deal
he made with God who does not exist except
as flakes of bone amid the ashes of
a man who sinned more than was sinned against,
who seems now barely to have been a man,
a man-boy I would reach back in time and touch
on his shoulder, and when he turned around
I'd lock his eyes to mine and ask him please
to run away alone, to leave his wife
and kids to pick among the shards of hope
for pocket change and bottle caps, for easy
money and easier claim on lives outside
the borders of Daddyland, where such as I

see nothing, hear nothing, know next to nothing,
yet are essential to the brazen story
of a fall from grace into a titular state
of deathward rest among the weathered stones.

The Word Made Mud: Interview with the Golem During Which Katrovas Attempts to Hire Him for the 25th Anniversary of the Prague Summer Program

The Golem, through his agent, agreed to meet me on the bank of the Vltava, below Vyšehrad, at 6 a.m. on a Friday. It was late fall; the sky was turning from black to gray, the moon was pale and almost full, and the air was crisp. The Golem climbed lugubriously from the river, stood dripping on the cement dock before the green bench, overlooking the water, on which I waited. The Golem, eight-feet tall and svelte (for a monster), dropped gently to his knees, sat back on his haunches, dipped his chin in silent salutation. He smelled of mellow rot.

KATROVAS: Thank you for agreeing to this interview, sir.

GOLEM: Where good men gather, vengeance sleeps.

KATROVAS: Your English is excellent.

GOLEM: The stars on still, clear nights have nothing to do with poignant endings.

KATROVAS: Well, be that as it may, you are your father's son.

GOLEM: Swans are nasty.

KATROVAS: And where indeed were you when the Nazis marched in?

GOLEM: All love is conditional to the extent that all walls are not.

KATROVAS: Well, given that you were born to protect, and that you failed so many, has your reading of Leviticus altered such that you now favor macrobiotics?

GOLEM: Hysterical laughter occupies every snowflake.

KATROVAS: In 1989, on this very day of the year, did you feel vindicated?

GOLEM: Time's march is through the hearts of heroes.

KATROVAS: And into what? Myth? History? Stupid question. The distinction is academic.

GOLEM: The laws of nature have neither spirit nor letter.

KATROVAS: And what of destiny?

GOLEM: Father was a man of God, though God was not the father of accountants.

KATROVAS: Were you, have you ever been, a member of the Communist Party?

GOLEM: Čapek or Kafka is a false choice.

KATROVAS: Do you understand yourself to be a Christ figure?

GOLEM: Gone are the days of missed opportunities dipping into the glorious realm of compassionate rage.

KATROVAS: But, if poetry is dead, is compassion an amusement park out of season?

GOLEM: Defenestration is the pastime of cowards.

KATROVAS: When the right hand doesn't know that the left one is clapping, do demographic processes get gummed up in good intentions?

GOLEM: Our poets washed windows.

KATROVAS: Thus the soul is revealed. But what of irony?

GOLEM: Thus the soul is revealed.

KATROVAS: Every July for the past twenty-five years, we've brought American and other English-speaking writers to Prague because you, the post-Apocalyptic muse, still do the breaststroke in the Vltava at dawn.

GOLEM: I'm a sucker for sass, a true believer in the soufflé that rises to the fear of extinction.

KATROVAS: Will you join us this summer? We'll pay you three thousand crowns for a forty-minute lecture on sleeping under water.

GOLEM: You'll have to work that out with my agent.

KATROVAS: Who's your favorite poet?

GOLEM: Groucho Marx. And a kid in Olomouc who composes in a Sanskrit argot.

KATROVAS: Who's your favorite playwright?

GOLEM: Havel and Shakespeare, not necessarily in that order.

KATROVAS: Who's your favorite novelist?

GOLEM: Kundera and that kid in Olomouc who's a switch-hitter.

KATROVAS: Verse and prose fiction?

GOLEM: Prose verse and lyrical fiction.

KATROVAS: As the sun rises, you grow more distinct.

GOLEM: As the sun rises, so do you.

KATROVAS: Does a writer's life have purpose?

GOLEM: It has porpoise.

KATROVAS: Is that a joke, a bit of Golem humor?

GOLEM: It's an aquatic mammal, poetry in motion.

KATROVAS: You have, for the past quarter century, blessed the Prague Summer Program. Do you still bless our enterprise? Do you still approve of English-language writers converging on Prague in July?

GOLEM: I don't approve, but still I bless.

KATROVAS: Your blessing is the high-octane fuel of our ambition.

GOLEM: I'm sleepy.

KATROVAS: The sun is rising. You get the last word.

GOLEM: I am the last word made flesh.

KATROVAS: Mud. You are composed of mud.

GOLEM: I am the word made mud.

The Golem rose from his haunches, saluted the dawn, and cannonballed into the midst of gathered swans that seemed barely to notice. The splash was an amphibrach.